BUSINESSES YOU CAN START NOW

Start your own business with little money and/or little time.

Jean Atkins

Businesses You Can Start Now

ISBN-13: 978-1499694970

ISBN-10: 1499694970

Dedication:

To all those who believe in this dream of owning
your own business and go after it.

Thank you to all the friends and business owners
who provided their wealth of knowledge and information.

Introduction

There are many reasons why you are reading this book...maybe you are unhappy in your current job and longing for a change, maybe you are unemployed and tired of waiting for someone to hire you or maybe you just want to take control of your destiny.

For many the problem with starting your own business is lack of startup capital and for many they are not able to get by without an income even for a short period of time. This book addresses that with several businesses you can start while still working a regular job. Many can be started on part-time basis for those who just want to supplement their income or those who need their current full-time salary while building their cash flow.

By conducting interviews of business owners and researching the opportunities out there this book provides you with a large selection of businesses that can be started with a small amount of capital and/or limited time. You need to work smart and you will have to work hard but you can achieve your dream of having your own business and taking control of your life. With the right plan it is possible for you build a very profitable and successful business.

Two of the biggest obstacles that many have to overcome are fear and time. When you work a full-time job the last thing you want to do after hours and on the weekend is work even more. But if you can find the passion in going after what you want and learn to have fun with it then it won't feel so much like "work". Fear is also a huge challenge...the fear of losing money, the fear of failure. But there is no reward without risk and no greater reward than achieving your dreams by overcoming fear.

If you put that fear aside, create a plan and follow through then you can make this happen. Start slowly, understand your business and learn from mistakes. Be prepared to work hard, be patient and move forward in achieving success.

Table of Contents

BUSINESSES YOU CAN START NOW

Are you ready...

Foreword

As a kid I wanted to make money and was always thinking of ways I could do that...I did the typical things, had a lemonade stand, collected cans, then babysitting. Then started working a part-time job in high school and knew I wanted more.

Eventually I started trying different ideas for starting my own business and had success by taking a passion of mine and turning it into a business which was photography. First I took a job for a school photography company to learn some business basics. Then branched out on my own doing sports teams and sporting events. Eventually I started doing some weddings and finally had a successful business.

Now I'm working on another passion, writing; so I'm combining my passion for being a business owner with my creative passion of writing and here we are.

If you have a passion and a desire to be your own boss, go after it; you may and probably will suf-

fer some setbacks but keep going and you will succeed and will find tremendous satisfaction for
achieving your dream.

Chapter One

GETTING STARTED – The Basics

The first step of course is deciding what business will work best for you; one that you can feel passionate about and utilize your skills.

As you go through the businesses described in this book you want to look at what would you enjoy doing every day? Look at your strengths and weaknesses and determine what you will enjoy doing every day. As you read through each of the businesses make a note of those that interest you and the reasons why you like it. Consider things such as do you like working with your hands, are you creative or do you have technology skills.

Here are some questions to ask yourself:
What are your major strengths?
How is your capacity to make decisions?
How hard are you willing to work?
Do you have the ability to take initiative?
How much time can you devote each week to your business in the first 6 months? And what days/hours can you devote to starting your business?

The kind of schedule you have can affect the business you start; for example, if you want to start a housecleaning business you will need to

1

have week days available to clean the houses. So if you need to keep a job while starting your business then having a Monday-Friday 8am-5pm job will conflict with this type of business.

You will also want to look at the market available to you and the type of consumers you want to reach. It is better to start out with a small specific market or "niche" market then expand as you grow. Don't expect to be the next big thing making a fortune within a few months; set short term realistic goals.

Consider if you want to provide a service or a product? A service type business requires less capital since you do not need inventory but it also typically requires a skill. There are some product provider businesses that do not require much capital; especially if you have a wholesale provider that will drop ship the product. Then you can focus on the marketing and sales of the product without having to spend money on inventory. It is important to choose a product or service that there is a demand for in your target market.

Business Plan

Once you determine your business the next step is to prepare a business plan. There are tools available to help you put together a business plan, some more detailed than others. Many think you only need a business plan if you are going to apply for a business loan or try to get funding from an investor but this is not true. You need a business plan so your vision is clear on how you are going to launch your business and follow specific goals.

Initially it can be a very simple business plan; define your business, your marketing plan and how much money you will need. Then as your business grows you can develop a more detailed and comprehensive plan which can be used to get funding or a credit line. As you grow you will also want to redefine your goals and marketing.

Know your numbers and include them in your plan; what is the cost of each product or service and what will be your target price point. Determine what your total expenses will be and deduct that from your set price to get a true sense of what your profit will be. Make sure you don't price yourself out of a profit but maintain a competitive price for strong sales.

All of this should be included in your business plan and adjusted or updated when needed.

Market Research

An important step in launching your business is doing market research; you need to know who your target market is and how to reach them. What you need to consider is:

Who are your primary customers?
What area or region are they in?
What is your target age demographic?
What is the income range of your target customers?
Any other specifics (i.e. ethnicity, career, homeowners, etc.)?

Keep in mind that market research isn't a perfect science but can be helpful in determining your marketing strategy. Understanding what your customers want and how to approach them is why market research is important.

You also want to research your competitors; details about their products/services, look at what their prices are, what kind of guarantees do they offer and their customer service. Also sign up for their newsletter if they offer one and check out their website. Ask your friends and family if they have used a competitor and find out what they liked about them and what they didn't like. The more you know about your competitors the more you can differentiate yourself from them while being competitive.

Legal Structure

First keep in mind these are guidelines and not meant to be legal advice. There are resources available for legal advice such as non-profit legal-aid centers and a great resource is your local SCORE chapter (www.score.org). SCORE is a non-profit association dedicated to helping small businesses through education and mentorship. Because their mentors are volunteers they are able to provide services at no cost and other classes and seminars for very low costs. The mentors are mostly retired business people with various areas of expertise and are a great source for you to utilize. When you contact your local chapter let them know what type of information you need help with such as business structure, accounting or legal related assistance, marketing, and they will connect you with a mentor. Plan on several visits with the same or different mentors depending on their areas of expertise; this is an invaluable tool at your disposal.

You will need to determine what legal form you will take for your business. The form of your business will affect your tax liability and they include:

> Sole Proprietorship
> Partnerships
> Corporation
> LLC (Limited Liability Corporation)

Starting out you will probably select a Sole Proprietorship or Partnership if you are launching this business with a partner. Then as your business grows you can form a Corporation or LLC which are more complicated but offer advantages with taxes and liability.

Sole Proprietorship

A sole proprietorship is the simplest type of business organization; it's for a single business owner. If you are a sole proprietor or a general partnership it is a good idea to obtain an official "doing business as" name authorization (a "DBA") but not always required (check with your state on these requirements). This is obtained from the county by filing a form and paying a small fee. There are also services that will file your DBA online for a small fee. If you form a corporation or LLC then you do not need to also file for a business name.

Before finalizing the name you want to use also check if the domain name is available or something close you can then register that domain name. You don't want to decide on a business name, register it then find out someone else already has the domain name. Because even if you don't have a website in the beginning you will need one eventually, they are a necessity for any business and much easier to have than you may think.

You also will want to check your local corporation commission to determine if a business license is required. Additionally you can use your personal social security number or it is very easy to obtain an EIN or Tax ID number with IRS; this can be done on their website and although it will be tied to your social security number it provides you with a separate number for filing taxes for your business.

It is also a good idea to open a separate business checking account to keep track of your finances. You will want to keep track of your business expenses and revenue for tax reasons.

Partnerships

If you are starting a business with one or more individuals then you will want to look at creating a partnership. A general partnership is created when two or more create a business and will jointly own the assets, profits and losses.

The advantage of a partnership is that with more than one owner the business can benefit from the resources of all in the partnership. The disadvantage is that all partners are still personally liable for the losses and other obligations of the business. This means if one of the partners commits to a loan or agreement on behalf of the business then all partners are responsible.

No matter what the relationship is with partners it is a good idea to have a written agreement that defines the partnership and the responsibilities and limitations of each partner. Include in this agreement:

- The responsibility of each partner

- How much money each partner is contributing / percentage of ownership

- How business decisions will be made

- How profit and losses are divided by each partner

- How the partnership will be dissolved if necessary

- The partnership agreement should also include stipulations on what happens if a partner dies or wants to leave the partnership so that a partner can sell its interest.

Corporations

Businesses may choose from a variety of corporate entities, based on their needs. A corporation is more complicated than a sole proprietorship or a partnership because there is stock involved. However, it has certain advantages that may make it worth considering as a business form.

A corporation is considered a separate legal entity. For this reason, stockholders can't be held liable for losses of the business except under extreme conditions when the "corporate veil" is pierced. But unless laws are actually broken, this is a very unlikely scenario.

One or more persons may own a corporation. Below are useful descriptions.

General Corporation

A general corporation, also known as a "C" corporation, is the most common corporate structure. A general corporation may have an unlimited number of stockholders. Consequently, it is usually chosen by those companies planning to have more than 30 stockholders or large public stock offerings. Since a corporation is a separate legal entity, a stockholder's personal liability is usually limited to the amount of investment in the corporation and no more.

Close Corporation

A close corporation is most appropriate for the individual starting a company alone or with a small number of people. There are a few significant differences between a general corporation and a close corporation. A close corporation limits stockholders to a maximum of 30. In addition, many close corporation statutes require that the directors of a close corporation must first offer the shares to existing stockholders before selling to new stockholders. Not all states recognize close corporations.

Subchapter S Corporation

A Subchapter S Corporation is a general corporation that has elected a special tax status with the IRS after the corporation has been formed. Subchapter S corporations are most appropriate for small business owners and entrepreneurs who prefer to be taxed as if they were still sole proprietors or partners.

When a general corporation makes a profit, it pays a federal corporate income tax on the profit. If the company also declares a dividend, the stockholders must report the dividend as personal income and pay more taxes.

S Corporations avoid this "double taxation" (once at the corporate level and again at the personal level) because all income or loss is reported only once on the personal tax returns of the stockholders.

For many small businesses, the S Corporation offers the best of both worlds, combining the tax advantages of a sole proprietorship or partnership with the limited liability and enduring life of a corporate structure.

S Corporation Restrictions

To elect S Corporation status, your corporation must meet specific guidelines.

- All stockholders must be citizens or permanent residents of the United States.
- The maximum number of stockholders for an S Corporation is 75.
- If an S Corporation is held by an "electing small business trust," then all beneficiaries of the trust must be individuals, estates or charitable organizations. Interests in the trust cannot be purchased.
- S Corporations may only issue one class of stock.
- No more than 25 percent of the gross corporate income may be derived from passive income.
- Not all domestic general business corporations are eligible for S Corporation Status.

For more detailed information about these changes and other aspects regarding S Corporation status, contact your accountant, attorney or local IRS office.

Limited Liability Company (LLC)
A Limited Liability Company is not a corporation, but it offers many of the same advantages. Many small business owners and entrepreneurs prefer LLC because they combine the limited liability protection of a corporation with the "pass through"" taxation of a sole proprietorship or partnership.

LLC have additional advantages over corporations:

- LLC allow greater flexibility in management and business organization.

- LLC do not have the ownership restrictions of S Corporations, making them ideal business structures for foreign investors.

- LLC accomplish these aims without the IRS' restrictions of an S Corporation.

- LLC are now available in all 50 states and Washington, D.C.

The shareholders of a corporation have control through their power to elect a board of directors, who hire the officers of the corporation. The shareholder with the majority number of shares will be able to control all corporate decisions. So if one shareholder owns 51% or more then that shareholder effectively controls the business.

The officers of the corporation who are chosen by the board of directors (who are chosen by the shareholders) are responsible for running the day-to-day business of the corporation.

If you are an employee in your corporation there are two ways to be paid; you can receive a salary or you can receive a dividend (distribution of profits) or a combination. There are tax implications so you will want to make sure that you are distributing the earnings in a way that will minimize tax liability.

The most important reason for you to incorporate your business is that a corporation is its own legal person, separate from its owners. This means you cannot be held personally liable for debts of the corporation except under extreme circumstances. Therefore the only risk is that of what the investors have invested in the company. This is unless the shareholders personally sign an obligation for the corporation then they are legally responsible.

To get started with doing business as a corporation, you will need to comply with the formal laws of the state that you form in order to create the corporation. The stockholders need to agree on a number of items. These include:

- The name of the corporation
- The total number of shares of stock the corporation can sell or issue (known as "authorized shares").
- The number of shares of stock each of the owners will have when the corporation is formed.
- The amount of money or other property each owner will contribute in return for the shares of stock.
- The business in which the corporation will engage.
- Who the directors and officers of the corporation will be.

- What the articles of incorporation will say.

Because your corporation will be a legal entity separate from its owners, it will need a separate bank account and separate records. The money and property that the shareholders pay to buy their stock, and the assets and money that are earned by the corporation, are owned by the corporations and not by the shareholders.

If you have other questions regarding LLC or other types of corporations be sure to speak with a qualified legal and/or financial adviser.

Chapter Two

MARKETING STRATEGIES

For any business you will want to have a marketing strategy which identifies your target customer. That way the business can design its product, prices, distribution, promotional effort and services towards the target market.

A successful marketing campaign is one that generates more in sales or profit than you spend; therefore you must focus on a marketing campaign that will maximize profits.

There are two ways to segment your target marketing; they are:

- Geographical - identifying the needs of customers in a particular geographical area;
- Customer – identifying those who are most likely to buy your product or service.
- Your marketing plan should identify the segments you want to focus on and how to reach those markets.

First you want to look at demographics; this includes characteristics such as:

- Sex
- Age
- Education
- Geographic location
- Home ownership or renters

- Marital status
- Household income
- Ethnic or religious background
- Job classification

Other classifications include:
- Price vs. value perception
- Quality of the product or service
- Trust in the company
- Benefit of the product or service

Market Position

You can't be all things to everyone so you want to focus on your target market. Prospective customers will recognize your unique benefits or advantages over your competition if your marketing is properly positioned. The way to market your product or service successfully is to identify the market segments you want to reach; then determine what marketing tactics will maximize your profits. It is important to give your product or service brand identification.

You want to position your business so that you can set yourself apart from your competitors while attracting your target market. Some strategies include:

- Position on specific features: if your product or service has some unique feature that offers an unusual value then you can market that feature and set yourself apart.

- Position on benefits: typically this is the most effective strategy because you can help your customers envision what your product or service can do for them. If a customer understands how your product or service can benefit them they will come to you.

- Position on specific uses: this can be an effective marketing strategy by establishing yourself to a niche market; by focusing on specific segments you can put yourself in that segment as a leader.

- Hybrid position: you may want to incorporate elements from several positions; such as marketing on specific features and the specific uses. This doesn't mean you just throw out any and all marketing positions to see what sticks; you will still focus on your specific marketing position and tactics and have a purpose with your marketing.

Your marketing plan needs to contain four key elements combined to make one seamless marketing effort. These elements are:
- Product and/or Service
- Promotion
- Price
- Distribution

The plan will feature the product(s) and service provided; promotion strategies such as advertising, direct marketing, public relations efforts, specialized promotions and direct sales. A well thought-out pricing plan is important; if your prices are too cheap it can affect your profits. You want to also determine how you want to present yourself as either a discount provider or a premium provider...are you a Hyundai or Mercedes? Then the last element of distribution is how you plan to sell your product; will you be selling through a retailer or direct to the customer.

After implementing a marketing plan you will need to evaluate its effectiveness and make adjustments if needed. Again the goal of your marketing plan is to determine how your product or service will solve a problem or fills a customer's need then communicate that to your target market.

There are several ways to begin your marketing plan at a minimal cost such as using flyers, social media and direct email marketing.

If your target market is in a specific location then utilizing flyers in that location can be effective. However if you use this method of marketing make sure the flyers are professional and gets your message out in a easy to read and understand manner. Start with an eye-catching headline then briefly describe your product or service in a manner that will peak their interest and end with your contact information and website. If you are selling a service then you are selling you...so include a photo and promote yourself as the brand. And try to communicate a sense of urgency; such as a special price or gift being offered for a limited time.

Social media such as Facebook and Twitter are an inexpensive and effective method for getting your business name out there. Create a profile for your business and get all your friends and family on there then promote, promote, promote. Another method is blogging about subjects that are related to your business or products. There are books available to help you specifically with using social media and blogging to promote your business.

Email marketing is another method you can use especially if you have a specific target audience; there are email lists you can purchase for specific customers such as homeowners, jobs/careers, income levels, etc. Be willing to spend a little money to get a good list, a cheap list will probably contain outdated emails which are a waste of money. So spend the money on a quality email list for your target market then use a service provider that handles email campaigns and manages your lists such as Constant Contact or Mail-Chimp.

Cross promoting with other businesses can be effective by working with a company that compliments your business and vice versa so that you can promote each other. For example if you have a house cleaning business then approach a pet sitting business in your area about working together to promote each other.

For all of these marketing strategies be sure you provide a phone number that if you are not able to answer has a professional voicemail. And it's important that you handle the response to your marketing in a professional and timely manner either by phone or email.

And finally in order to give your business credibility and to compete you need to have a website. It's more affordable and easier to set up a website than many realize. You will need to obtain a domain name which you can purchase at GoDaddy.com. In fact when naming your business you may want to check that the domain name is available first. You don't want to select a business name only to find out later that the domain name is already taken by another business with the same name. There are several web-hosting providers that make it easy to set up your website; here are a few:

GoDaddy > www.GoDaddy.com
1&1 > www.1and1.com
iPage > www.iPage.com
Yahoo > www.SmallBusiness.Yahoo.com
JustHost > www.justhost.com
Volusion > www.volusion.com (for an online store)

A high-quality site-builder is essential to developing a successful website. When considering your options for free site-builder tools, you want to make sure that you choose one which offers you the most advanced template designs, attractive template variety, the most structural control and the best user-friendly interface. First, take a look at the template designs available.

Many free website builders come with a generous selection of template designs, but many are outdated. If you want to be successful on the internet today, you need your website to look slick and current. Second, consider how much structural control you have through their website editor. It's your website, and you should be able to ensure that it is constructed according to the layout and map you prefer. Lastly, it is essential that the site-builder be intuitive and easy to use. Because, what good is a free website builder if the interface is so confusing that you spend days just trying to figure out how to upload a header logo? Whether you are a seasoned website developer or working on building your first website, you want to make sure that your Website builder is as user-friendly as possible.

Chapter Three

ACCOUNTING, FINANCIAL MANAGEMENT AND TAXES

An efficient accounting system for your business is vital for your overall success and profitability. Eventually you will want to retain an accountant to help you with your business finances and taxes but that's usually not feasible in the beginning; here are some basics to get you started and as mentioned earlier there are valuable resources at SCORE to also help you with finances and accounting.

Information Leads to Profits

The reason for having an accounting system is to track, record, and provide financial information in a manner that is easy to analyze and assess. It produces useful information that tells specific things about the company.

The type of information you need from your accounting system is the kind that will allow you to have a "snap shot" of your company's financial condition with a short-term and long-term picture. Some popular accounting software systems such as QuickBooks will help with this but do require knowledge of the software; there are classes you can take to learn how to use it.

There are principal elements of all accounting systems; if you understand how debits and credits work then you will understand the accounting system.

Every accounting entry in the general ledger contains both a debit and a credit...all debits must equal all credits. If they don't the entry is out of balance so the account will not balance. Therefore the accounting system must have a mechanism to ensure that all entries balance. Most automated accounting systems won't let you enter an out-of-balance entry and will signal you that an error has been made.

Depending on what type of account you are dealing with, a debit or credit will either increase or decrease the account balance. Some basic accounting books or classes will help.

So remember that for every increase in one account there is an opposite and equal decrease in another. That is the backbone of accounting, everything else is just a variation on the same principal.

Income and Expenses

If you have more than one department or area of income it is a good idea to create an income account for each, that way you can better track from where your income is coming from. This is done in your accounting system, then you will add them together for total revenue.

The same can be done for expenses; by creating separate expense accounts you can track each type of expense. Typical expense accounts include:

- Salaries/Wages
- Communications/Technology
- Utilities
- Rent
- Maintenance
- Repairs
- Loans/Interest
- Depreciation

Other Financial Details

As part of your accounting system, it is also a good idea to have financial statements that you can use for things like seeking credit or attracting investors for your business.

BALANCE SHEET – this is a snapshot of the company's financial position; these are the assets and liabilities of the company.

Assets include:

- Cash

- Accounts Receivable

- Inventory

- Real Estate

- Equipment

- Vehicles

Liabilities include:
- Loans

- Equipment Leases

- Accounts Payable

As the owner, the equity you have is the balance after you take the assets and subtract the liabilities; this is also known as the net worth of the company.

Analyzing the balance sheet periodically will provide you with important information on the financials of your company. You can evaluate things like inventory and cash flow.

Proper management of assets and liabilities are important to your business. Break them down into current (short-term) and fixed (long-term). Short-term assets and liabilities are those that come into play within a year; as a low budget start-up you probably won't have any long term assets or liabilities for a while.

INCOME STATEMENT – an income statement is also called a profit and loss statement. This shows the income and expenses over a period of time or how much money the company has made. Keep in mind that income and cash flow are not necessarily the same thing; if you provide sales or service on credit that is counted as income but if you are not able to collect than that affects your cash flow.

For this it is extremely important to be thorough with invoicing and collections. Make sure you are organized with your invoices and monthly statements. As a small business, billing at the beginning of the work cycle will allow you to maintain a positive cash flow. But in some cases it is necessary to bill after services are provided so being prompt with collections is important.

As a new business owner, remember the importance of carefully extending credit and aggressively collecting on accounts. Don't wait until cash flow is a problem to start being proactive with collections.

TAXES – as a business owner there are various taxes that you can be responsible for; these include payroll taxes plus state and federal taxes.

Each business structure has different income tax requirements regarding filing dates, forms required, tax rates and calculations. The IRS provides lists of the various business taxes and forms required for each legal structure.

Most will be a Sole Proprietorship which means you will include the income and expenses with your personal tax return. If it's a Partnership then each partner includes their share of the income or loss on their own tax return. If you form a corporation or LLC then additional tax forms are required; you should consult a professional tax accountant.

Chapter Four

MANAGING YOUR BUSINESS

Time Management

When you don't have work lined up, figuring out how much to time to dedicate to your marketing efforts is easy...as much as possible.

It's important to spend time each day or each week to market yourself, your services, and/or your products. Everyone is a little different, for some it's most productive to spend the same time each day on your business...to have a routine and schedule. For others they want to spend every free moment on the business. But you need to determine what works for you but make sure you put in the time to make it a success or it will wither and die.

Practice the following techniques to become the master of your own time:

1. Carry a schedule and record all your thoughts, conversations and activities for a week. This will help you understand how much you can get done during the course of a day and where your precious moments are going. You'll see how much time is actually spent producing results and how much time is wasted on unproductive thoughts, conversations and actions.

2. Any activity or conversation that's important to your success should have a time

assigned to it. To-do lists get longer and longer to the point where they're unworkable. Appointment books work. Schedule appointments with yourself and create time blocks for high-priority thoughts, conversations, and actions. Schedule when they will begin and end. Have the discipline to keep these appointments.

3. Plan to spend at least 50 percent of your time engaged in the thoughts, activities and conversations that produce most of your results.

4. Schedule time for interruptions. Plan time to be pulled away from what you're doing. Take, for instance, the concept of having "office hours." Isn't "office hours" another way of saying "planned interruptions?"

5. Take the first 30 minutes of every day to plan your day. Don't start your day until you complete your time plan. The most important time of your day is the time you schedule to schedule time.

6. Take five minutes before every call and task to decide what result you want to attain. This will help you know what success looks like before you start. And it will also slow time down. Take five minutes after each call and activity to determine whether your desired result was achieved. If not, what was missing? How do you put what's missing in your next call or activity?

7. Put up a "Do not disturb" sign when you absolutely have to get work done.

8. Practice not answering the phone just because it's ringing and e-mails just because
   they show up. Disconnect instant messag-
   ing. Don't instantly give people your attention unless it's absolutely crucial in your
   business to offer an immediate human response. Instead, schedule a time to answer
   email and return phone calls.
9. Block out other distractions like Facebook
   and other forms of social media unless you
   use these tools to generate business.
10. Remember that it's impossible to get eve-
    rything done. Also remember that odds are
    good that 20 percent of your thoughts,
    conversations and activities produce 80
    percent of your results.

Goals

How does goal setting translate into moving your forward with your business? First, your
goals should be focused, that means specific.

Identify your top 10 goals and ask yourself
which ones will do the most to move your business forward in the coming year. Focus on the top
two or three goals then move on. The key to
achieving goals and to managing your day is to
look at the tasks you set for yourself each day in
terms of urgency and importance. Then take them
one by one continually move forward.

Inventory Management

Depending on the nature of your business, if you have inventory then management and keeping accurate records of your inventory is important. Basic records should include the date purchased, vendor, purchase price, date sold and sale price. This will also allow you to track your best sellers and concentrate on stocking these items for the greatest profit. By getting rid of your slow movers you will be able to lower inventory balance and improve cash flow. Although be careful of not having enough inventory to fulfill orders which could interrupt cash flow.

Often new business owners do not manage inventory well; either buying too much or too little. They may not properly keep track and lose control of their inventory. Here are some basic inventory rules:

- Restrict access to inventory; remember inventory is money.

- Check inventory frequently with your records; spot checks allow you to stay on top of your inventory.

- Concentrate on the fast moving products and reduce quantity of the slow movers.

- Work with your suppliers on lead times for your orders so that you can control your inventory.

A good solid inventory management system will allow you to maximize profits and improve cash flow.

Practice smart accounting as discussed previously as that is key to managing your business and making successful. Marketing your business and yourself are also vital to making your business successful.

Licenses / Permits

When starting your business and as it grows be sure you know what licenses and/or permits are needed to run your business. As discussed earlier you will probably start as a Sole Proprietor and will obtain your EIN from the IRS; but if you are operating your business under a business or fictitious name (dba – doing business as) then you may need to register your name with your city, county and/or state. Requirements for this vary by state, many require you to register with the county office and pay a small fee. When opening a business bank account some may require a fictitious name certificate. If you are set up as a corporation or LLC then you do not need to also file for a fictitious name.

Also contact your city's business license department to find out the requirements for a business license which grants you the right to operate in that city (and requires a small fee). You can also check with city about zoning laws for operating your business out of your home.

If you are dealing with food you will also need to contact the local health department about obtaining a permit. And if serving liquor, wine or beer a license is required in most states.

Contact your local city and/or state government office to find out what licenses you need and request the necessary forms.

Insurance

A common mistake made by new business owners is lack of insurance. The basics you need to look at obtaining coverage are: general liability, auto and property/casualty and workers' compensation for when you hire employees. Check with your local government office and your insurance agent to determine what coverage you need and how much.

There are other insurance policies to consider as a business owner such as Life insurance and Disability insurance.

Then review your insurance needs each year as you grow.

Employees

Start your business with one employee, you, then as you grow look at adding another employee. When you are ready to add an employee you will need to know and understand the labor laws in your state and payroll expenses.

The employees you hire can make or break your business. When you get to the point you are overwhelmed and need to hire someone do not get too anxious and hire the first person that walks in. Consider what type of position you need to hire someone to fill, consider the money you can pay and make sure it fits your needs and your budget.

When hiring make sure you know the labor laws in your state and understand payroll requirements and the records you must keep as an employer. You can also look at hiring contract labor or from a temporary agency to start.

Keep in mind that good management skills can turn even average workers into a winning team. You will need to know how to interact with your team members in a way that will be positive and will motivate them to want to do their best. Four steps that will boost everyone's productivity are:

- Invest in your top performers
- Don't manage people, manage objectives
- Treat people (employees) well
- Don't hang on to the weak links

Set high standards for your business, your employees and yourself. When higher standards are set, your employees will feel greater pride in being a part of an above-average organization. Most will want to live up to that standard of excellence, those who don't aren't the employees you need.

Growth

As your business grows you may need a more comprehensive business plan. You might need a more detailed, formal plan in order to:

- Obtain outside funding

- Increase your credit line from suppliers
- Find management support for your operation and finances
- Increase your promotion and marketing efforts
- Expand your inventory or space
- Revise your business goals and objectives

So as you move ahead in this exciting new adventure that will potentially change your life, develop the right frame of mind where you will be prepared to do whatever it takes to succeed. By doing this, being focused and doing the legwork necessary, you will maximize your chances of owning your own successful business.

The most critical choice you will make in our quest to own and operate your own business will be what type of business you choose to establish. It's important that you select a business that you will be able to successfully operate and one that you will enjoy owning because it allows you to achieve your personal goals.

One of the greatest rewards of owning your own business is having a life where getting up and going to work is not a repulsive idea. You will want to be working in a business where you can apply your best assets so that you can maximize your return on your most valuable asset...YOU!

Now let's review several businesses that you can start with a limited budget and some that can be started with limited time.

Chapter Five

BUSINESSES YOU CAN START NOW

ARTS AND CRAFTS

Candle making is a great craft to learn. You can often easily sell the candles at local shops and also through websites like Etsy.com.

Jewelry design is another craft if you have a good eye for detail work and a lot of patience it can be quite profitable. As with other crafts, there are many opportunities to sell such items through local gift shops or at sites like etsy.

Knitting / crocheting / quilting Skilled at creating blankets and sweaters? There's a *huge* market for these types of items – even better, you can usually make them in your spare time whenever you have it. As always, local shops and places like etsy are great places to go to sell such items.

Set your price by determining the cost of materials and the minimum hourly rate you want to make. Adjust your price by factoring in the demand for your craft and other competing products. Market your products through arts and craft shows, on a website, at online auction sites, at gift stores or at home parties. And you can lower your costs by purchasing supplies wholesale. Find wholesalers by researching products online.

The great thing about most craft businesses is that they are ideally suited to operate as a home-based business. If that's your plan, look around your home and map out where you will store inventory, take care of the business details like bill paying and make your craft product. If you're planning to rent a shop, this expense needs to factored into your cost of doing business.

Skills/Licenses Needed:
Being skillful with arts and crafts of course is needed for this type of business. You will need a tax ID license in order to buy from wholesalers.

Other Resources:
www.festivalnet.com
www.etsy.com
www.opensky.com

BOOKKEEPING

For those with bookkeeping/accounting experience can start a bookkeeping business from home; potential clients are small businesses and other at-home businesses. Many small businesses do not have the finances or need for a full-time bookkeeper so this could be a service you can provide. If you do not have experience there are many community schools or online courses available.

Market yourself as a professional bookkeeper who will provide a custom accounting system to meet your client's needs. Prepare a presentation book with your skills, qualifications and accounting systems. You can also market additional services such as preparing loan applications, income tax preparations, payroll, corporate documents and Notary Public services are a bonus.

To attract clients, one needs to advertise his or her bookkeeping business. This can be accomplished several ways, such as through distributing business cards in person or mailing brochures directly to businesses. Other options include contacting local media about ad placements and creating a business website. Depending on the location, many people also feel that word-of-mouth is an effective way to gain exposure and attract clients.

Having a professional look both personally and in your documents is very important. Always look your best when meeting with clients as first impressions can mean a lot. Be sure to keep quality looking business cards with you at all times. Matching letterhead and invoices are a must because they project a true business-like image to your clients. And make sure your clients can reach you easily. Some people like to use email or texting and some prefer to call and talk on the phone. You should have an email address that is used only for business and sounds professional. Organization skills are also important to keep up track of your schedule. The more clients you take on, the more demands will be placed on your time, and you want to avoid the embarrassment of missed appointments or failing to file documents on time.

You can offer your services on a weekly, monthly or annual plan and be willing to customize to the needs of your clients.

Skills/Licenses Needed:

Knowledge of taxes, financial reports such as Income Statements and payroll processing is necessary; plus knowledge of QuickBooks and other accounting programs is important. Any certifications or degrees in accounting will boost your credibility.

Other Resources:

www.aipb.org (AIPB) American Institute of Professional Bookkeepers

CARPET CLEANING SERVICE

Because this a service you provide in the clients home or business this is one you can start from home with minimal investment. It's possible to rent the equipment as you need it until you have enough to purchase your own. Obtaining commercial clients such as offices, stores, restaurants or schools will give you a regular income but competition is tough. But the large amount of competition also means that there is a opportunity for you to get out there and get a share of the market; so you will need to get out there and make your name known and really sell yourself to get the business.

In addition to carpet cleaning you can offer additional services including:

- Carpet and hard floor cleaning

- Wood floor refinish and repair

- Upholstery cleaning

- Tile and grout cleaning

With this type of industry, it's usually price that will get you the jobs; customer service is also important but being competitive on pricing will get you the jobs so you can build your brand name. But good customer service and letting people know you are a small business that will give them personal service is also a way to market yourself.

Also in order to set yourself up as a professional you need to have thorough knowledge of how to clean, drying times, possible issues that can happen. You need to become an expert and show your knowledge to the client so they feel confident in your expertise.

As for pricing your services it varies according to cities and locations so price out the competitors in your area to come up with a competitive pricing plan. Make sure though to take your expenses into account so that you are not losing money.

Skills / Licenses Needed:

For this business there are no licenses needed; but this is a physical job so you will need to be able to handle the physicality and have some mechanical aptitude on handling equipment.

Other Resources:

http://professionalassociationofcleaningandrestoration.org (Professional Association of Cleaning and Restoration)

www.lmcca.org (Low Moisture Carpet Cleaners Association)

www.rugcarespecialists.org (Assoc of Rug Care Specialists)

CATERING

The catering business is one of the most lucrative and profitable home businesses with a high potential for expansion and growth. It is both financially rewarding and fun. Each catered event – whether birthday parties for children, breakfast in bed and intimate candlelight dinners for two, company dinner parties for 50 and wedding receptions involving a hundred or more guests — is a new experience and challenge with a new group of people.

Whether you cater events on a full-time or part-time basis, the opportunities are excellent. However, catering is a demanding work, requiring stamina, ability to work under pressure, and excellent interpersonal skills. Your success will greatly depend on your reputation. To build a good reputation in the business, you should be willing to work hard and the ability to work under pressure. This kind of entrepreneurial business is definitely growing and becoming more popular with people of all income levels.

In the catering business, you can start as small or as big as your wallet will allow. Your catering business can offer catering services for corporate events, meetings, holiday gatherings, picnics, weddings, family reunions, birthdays, graduations and more. Most caterers do the cooking on-site, either using their own facilities or equipment provided by the clients. However, you would still need to do some prep-work in your own kitchen facilities (e.g. pre-cutting vegetables, etc.)

To keep your initial costs down, you can opt to start your catering business by renting items. You may rent the use of kitchen facilities, china, utensils, tables, tablecloths and linens, serving equipment and other staples. There are plenty of vendors exist to help you pull together the perfect event — decorators, designers, event planners, florists, bakers, and rental companies for portable toilets, cooking equipment, tents, chairs, linens, tableware, glassware, and silverware. You can start buying your own equipment only when you have steady revenues. By renting equipment, facilities and supplies, you can use your first few months to build your reputation, develop some capital for investment and expansion and evaluate how much time and money you want to invest.

Skills / Licenses Needed:

You do not need special education or training to become a successful caterer. However, taking some courses at culinary institutes or vocational schools can significantly help improve the quality of your food offerings. Instead of taking cooking lessons, some caterers start out by working for one or more catering businesses to learn about the catering business and how the business works.

Caterers today have to be adept not only in satisfying the taste buds but also excel in food preparation. With the goal of wowing the socks off the clients, many caterers give ample focus on plate presentations, venue selection, and table decoration, among others.

Other Resources:
www.internationalcaterers.org
www.nace.net (National Association for
Catering and Events)

CHILD CARE SERVICE / DAYCARE

Starting a child care business in your home is a business that you can start with minimal funds but requires a great deal of responsibility. There is a difference between being a baby-sitter and running a child care service with several children that you are responsible for so you will want to be prepared.

First put together your business plan and determine the following:

- Maximum number of children

- Meals – providing lunch, snacks; being prepared for food allergies and restrictions

- Playtime space – is there suitable space for the children to play; is there an outdoor area for the kids to play; plan organized games.

- Medical – being CPR certified is a must; prepared to administer medication with the parent's written instruction.

- Paperwork – have forms prepared for every parent to complete that uses your service which includes their information and instructions as well as your procedures and policies (one should be to require payment up front).

- Equipment – note what expenses you will have in providing equipment such as toys, games, blankets, pillows, first-aid kits and food.

Also include in your business plan who your target market is which of course includes all families in your area but you may want to specifically target single parents; or depending on your home or location you could target parents who want a more catered experience for their child. If your home is modest and you live in a lower income area then you won't want to market to affluent parents, you will want to keep it modest and simple while offering quality service.

When it comes to someone's child it's not always the best price but the quality and service you can provide that will be a big factor in a parent's decision to choose you.

Offering Unique Service

Parent's want to know their children will be cared for and want to feel good about leaving their children with you; so position yourself as a caring and nurturing childcare provider. Have a plan you can promote to provide educational learning and exposure to culture such as art and music.

Another benefit you can offer would be to install a security camera system that allows the parents to view your location on a website. These do not cost much at a technology type store and will be a valuable service that sets you apart from many.

Skills/Licenses Needed:

Of course you need to have some experience with children and enjoy spending time with children; you also need a great deal of patience and a calm temperament...you can never lose your cool around the children. A basic understanding of child development and care is necessary; and as mentioned earlier it is important to be certified in CPR and have basic first aid knowledge.

Licensing and legal requirements vary by state so you will need to check your state laws on zoning ordinances, insurance requirements and licensing. Additionally check on facility requirements such as fire alarms, exits, and health standards for food preparation. Many of these laws may vary according to how many children are being cared for.

It is a good idea to check your homeowner's policy about adding a rider; discuss your needs with your insurance agent. Or it may be necessary to obtain a separate policy; you can check with the National Association for Family Day Care on their group policy.

Do your research and check what the daycare centers and child care providers are charging in your area; find out what services they provide so that you can determine a fair price for your service which will allow you a suitable profit margin.

Other Resources:

http://nrckids.org (The National Resource Center for Health and Safety in Child Care and Early Education) http://childcareaware.org/child-care-pro-viders (Childcare Aware)

CLEANING SERVICE

Today's busy families and households with their hectic schedules need more help with the housework making this an easy business to start and one that is in demand. This is a business with minimal startup capital needed but one that if you do not like cleaning then it's not for you.

With the demand growing, residential housecleaning has become one of the fastest growing businesses and is expected to increase in demand through the next five years. Another option is commercial cleaning which is a little more competitive business but can be very lucrative with a low initial investment; this is covered separately under Commercial Cleaning Service.

Also with housecleaning you will need to be available in the daytime during typical working hours which is when most clients want their house cleaned; whereas commercial cleaning you will need to work evenings and weekends.

In creating your company's marketing position you need to offer something special or unique to make yourself competitive. Typically price is one of the most effective ways to attract clients but also the customer service you provide can set yourself apart. Reliability and quality are the other two biggest features that clients look for in a cleaning service.

Your target market will be those who live in affluent and middle class residential housing; it's not just homeowners that hire cleaners but also renters and those in condominiums and apartments are using them more. Depending on whom your target client is you will market yourself differently; such as for someone in a middle-class neighborhood you will promote yourself as a dis-count service but for those in a more affluent neighborhood you will promote your quality and service.

Also for potential clients you are marketing yourself as a discount service you can offer an ad-ditional discounted price if they provide the clean-ing supplies versus you provide the supplies. This will save you some time and money so that you can pass that on to the client.

Ensure all advertisements, business cards, contracts, invoices or any other correspondence includes your license number so customers may verify your license with the appropriate governing body. Additionally, note in your service agree-ments or contracts that you're bonded as a house-cleaner and provide customers with information about who to contact in the event a job is not completed and how to seek reimbursement. This will provide that extra confidence in your clients that will separate you from the competition.

You will need basic cleaning supplies such as a vacuum, bucket, sponges, cleaning cloths, mop, broom, duster and other cleaning prod-ucts. As previously mentioned though some cli-ents may provide these supplies for a discounted rate.

Do your research and find out what clean-ers in your area or target area are charging and structure your pricing accordingly.

Skills / Licenses Needed:

Not everyone is skilled at cleaning so you need to have that skill of cleaning and paying attention to detail; also this is a physical job so being to perform the duties in a timely manner is essential. Look at your own home, if you keep it clean including the baseboards and other areas some may miss then you have the skill.

Since you will be working in homes and usually when the homeowner is gone it is a good idea to be licensed and bonded. Contact your local city, county and state governments to obtain information about licensing laws in your area, license requirements and licensing procedures. Some locations license housecleaners as service contractors, while others require only a general business license to operate in the specified area. Additionally, some locations may require you to hold a certain amount of insurance coverage or file a surety bond prior to being licensed.

Purchase a professional bond from your insurance agent or contact a surety insurance company. The amount of the bond will depend on the size and scope of your housecleaning business, or on local regulations, but usually bonds cover about $2,000 to $10,000 of customer reimbursement for an independent housecleaning contractor or small service business.

Other Resources:

www.suretybonds.com/janitorial-service-bonds.html

www.arcsi.org (Association of Residential Cleaning Services International)

COACHING SERVICE

Professional coaches provide an ongoing partnership designed to help clients produce fulfilling results in their personal and professional lives. Coach's help people improve their performances and enhance the quality of their lives.

There are different types of coaches which include:

- Life Coach
- Wellness or Health Coach
- Corporate or Executive Coach

The role of a coach is to perform the following services:

- Provide objective assessment and observations for the client's self-awareness
- Practice astute listening in order to garner a full understanding of the client's circumstances
- Encourage changes in thinking and/or lifestyle that reveal fresh perspectives, challenge blind spots in order to illuminate new possibilities, and support the creation of alternative scenarios

Your target market will be those that can afford private coaching and those open to coaching; potential clients include:

- o Business owners
- o Executives and managers
- o Artists
- o Writers
- o Athletes

- Weight issues
- Relationship issues

In order for a client to want to procure your services he or she will need to believe that you will be able to help them significantly improve your life. In order for you to do this you must communicate to potential clients that you will do any and all of the following for them:

- Create personal change that will cause positive life changes
- The changes will only be positive in nature
- Changes that are deep and substantial and not merely cosmetic
- Increased focus assisting with developing the right plans of action

Tips for getting started and attracting clients are:

- Offer free consultation and be prepared to provide your credentials
- Use tools like assessment programs, checklists and coaching models
- Initially consider taking on a client or two at no charge to develop legitimate references

As for supplies and equipment needed, there isn't much...basic office supplies such as computer, phone, email, business cards, etc.

Skills / Licenses Needed:

There are essentially no license require-ments in this field, but there are industry organiza-tions and schools that offer guidelines and provide training. Of course you will need to already have some skill or experience in the area of coaching you are going into. The more experience, back-ground and knowledge you have in the field you are serving as a coach the better for attracting and securing clients.

The International Coaching Federation (ICF) prescribes a set of minimum requirements at three levels for credentialing to allow one to use the title of Certified Coach (CC).

Other Resources:
www.thecoaches.com
www.coachinc.com/CoachU/
www.coachfederation.org
www.integrativenutrition.com
www.fowlerwainwright.com

COMMERCIAL CLEANING SERVICE

First and foremost, decide what you want to do with your commercial cleaning business. Do you want to clean small buildings or large buildings? Do you want to keep this business small or do you want to hire employees to do the work for or with you? This will determine what sort of buildings you are going to target.

There are many different areas of commercial cleaning. You can do small buildings such as banks, gyms, day cares, mom and pop shops or convenience stores. You can do small office buildings or large skyscraper buildings and schools. There are many options here. You will need to decide what you want to do.

If it is just you or just you and a partner, you may want to start small. Target smaller buildings that you can do by yourself. Then, when you get the feel for your business and want to hire help, target larger buildings.

Marketing is tricky in the beginning. There are many ways to market your business and some will work and some may not. The following is a list of the many things you can do to market a commercial cleaning business.

- Flyers / Mailings / Cold Calling
- Phone Book
- Website
- Online Advertising
- Newspaper

- Magazine
- Car Magnets
- Business Card Distribution
- Valpak
- Word of Mouth

You will need basic office equipment to run your business and you will need a bid proposal to submit to your clients. You will need to have one of these for your clients to sign. This will tell them what you are going to be doing and for how much. In addition to bid proposals, you will also need an invoice to submit to your clients monthly.

Also you can set yourself apart from many of your competitors by offering to pick up recyclables. Many cleaning services do not handle recyclables so offices are left to take it on themselves or not recycle at all.

Skills / Licenses Needed:
Liability insurance will be a requirement for commercial cleaning. They will want to see your insurance certificate and some businesses may even want you to carry a certain limit on your insurance policy. The most any business should need would be a $1Million policy, but usually $500k would suffice.

You can find commercial liability insurance through your local agents as well as by going to http://ww.netquote.com. Just click on business insurance and get a quote right there. This can be costly depending on where you live, but the average is around $500/year. So, be sure to shop around to get the best coverage and quote.

If you are going to hire employees or you have a partner, it would be a good idea to get a bond. A bond will protect your business against employee theft. Bonds are not expensive and most of your clients will want you to have one as well. Your local agent should be able to help you get one or you can get one at http://www.janitorialbonds.com/. You can also shop around for a bond. Just do a search on the web for a janitorial bond. There are many companies.

Other Resources:

www.issa.com (Worldwide Cleaning Industry Association)

www.bscai.org (Building Service Contractors Association International)

COMPUTER CONSULTANT

If you have skills and knowledge of computers and technology then you could start your own consulting business helping companies and individuals with their IT needs.

Services you could provide are systems integration and analysis, design and development, application or systems programming, training and education, technical writing, hardware design and development, installation, troubleshooting and repair, home set-up, etc.

Your primary targets are small businesses, organizations, private schools and individuals. To market yourself a website is a must. You can also attend conferences to network, mailings to target businesses, and advertise on Craigslist. It's important to provide great customer service as word of mouth referrals can be vital for your business. There is a great deal of competition in this field so you will need to set yourself apart. One way is to emphasize that you will educate the client on the benefits of the technology they purchased. And communicate with your clients on what you are doing and how long it will take; it's important to keep up communications if the job is taking longer or if there are unexpected issues.

Prepare your business plan and include what services you will provide, what hours you are working (will you offer 24 hour emergency calls) and your prices for service. Consider if you have to travel a distance to the client will you charge a fee for mileage. Check out competitors in your area for what services they provide and what do the charge.

Skills / Licenses Needed:

There are no specific licenses needed however there are several certifications you can obtain that will give you credibility.

As for skills you will need to have substantial technical knowledge and keep up with the changes in technology. There are also several areas of expertise that you can focus on.

Of course you will need to have a computer as basic equipment needed plus a wide inventory of computer programs so that you are familiar with them.

Other Resources:

www.icca.org (Independent Computer Consultants Association)

www.techservealliance.org (TechServe Alliance)

CONSULTANT

If you have skills and knowledge in a specific area then you can serve as a consultant; you will be able to examine situations, problems, organization for a client then evaluate and offer strategies for improvement.

As a consultant you will challenge the current situation to determine weaknesses and strengths. This in-depth analysis will result in recommendations for improvement.

Some fields that are common for consultants are:

- Marketing & Advertising

- Human Resources

- Safety / Protection

- Management

- Financial / Accounting

- Technology

- Inventory control

Your prime target will depend on your area of consulting, however typically your market will include businesses, schools, organizations, foundations and private individuals. Networking and referrals are critical so you will want to be active in organizations where potential clients are.

As a consultant you are selling yourself that you are an expert that can help solve a problem. You will want to emphasize your high professional standards of competence, objectivity and integrity.

Be prepared to give potential clients accurate and thorough estimates, budgets and timelines. Providing presentations to trade groups or business organizations for networking are excellent ways to obtain clients and become known as an expert in your field.

You can also offer to write articles on your area of expertise for industry or local publications and create a blog on your website.

Skills /Licenses Needed:

There are certain fields such as being a medical or legal consultant that would require licenses but most fields do not require a license. But again, certifications in your field are an advantage. And having an expert knowledge in the field you are performing as a consultant is necessary.

Keep in mind also that you will need to be able to maintain confidentiality and use proprietary client information only with the client's permission. An agreement of confidentiality should be included in your forms when being hired by a client.

Equipment and supplies are the basics such as computer, phone, business cards, etc. so you can create your office with minimal expense.

Do your research of consultants in your field of expertise to find out what services they provide and how much they charge.

Other Resources:

www.imcusa.org (Institute of Management Consultants)

www.centerforindependentconsulting.com (The Center for Independent Consulting)

COURIER SERVICE

As a local courier service you provide delivery services for local businesses on time and usually same day. Items that typically need to be delivered include letters, packages, and legal documents.

Depending on your location you would provide delivery by a motor vehicle but in some cases it can be done by bike messenger.

To determine where you will service and your price rates you will need to create a map of your delivery service area and break it down into zones of a fixed size. Then you can estimate the costs of delivery within each zone.

Some standard expenses to keep in mind:
- Transportation cost
- Fuel
- Insurance
- Communications (cell phone or two-way radio)

Any business is a potential customer but the banking and legal professions are prime targets. Typically these businesses work longer than eight-hour days and need to get documents out the same day so that is where your service is needed.

Legal documents often need to be originals, not faxed or electronic copies, which makes them a prime marketing target.

Do your research on what courier's charge in your area; because the profit margins are typically slim due to competitive prices what will set you apart is the service you provide. Services to offer include:

- Immediate pick-up
- Rapid delivery
- One-hour rush delivery service

To provide fast service make sure you research and know routes, distances and have a reliable navigation system. Build customer loyalty by providing extra customer service and occasional benefits to your regular customers.

This is a business you can start on your own then as it grows add extra couriers and continue to grow.

Skills / Licenses Needed:

Generally there are not any special licenses needed but check with your local authorities for specifics and on insurance requirements. There may be something to add to your automotive insurance policy.

As for equipment you will need a cell phone and reliable source of transportation.

Other Resources:

www.mcaa.com (Customized Logistics and Delivery Association)

www.couriermagazine.com (Courier Magazine)

ECOMMERCE

More and more people are opting to purchase goods online as it saves them time and money. Starting up your own ecommerce shop is a great way to supplement your income while meeting this growing demand for online purchases. You can sell just about anything through an ecommerce storefront, but it is a good idea to research the niche that you want to venture into.

The most successful ecommerce stores are those that cater to a specific audience. Other than buying products directly from manufacturers, storing them and then selling them to your customers, you can create your own unique products, arts and crafts to sell through an e-store.

Popular platforms such Esty and Pinterest can be a good place to start to display and sell your own handmade merchandise as described in the Arts & Crafts section. You may also use EBay, Amazon, Clickbank and Shopify to get started with online selling from home.

Start marketing and advertising your ecommerce site

You can start by submitting your site to major directories and secondary specialized directories in your industry/business category. Also, learn, research and dedicate some time, money and effort in keywords and sponsored search advertising.

Marketing and advertising would play a big part in the success of your ecommerce business.

To benefit from your ecommerce site, at minimum, you need to do some keyword and directory advertising. Every business situation requires a different marketing game-plan and advertising methods.

A good marketing team would analyze your industry, competitors, audiences, business environment and would suggest the best marketing strategy tailored to your business.

Skills / Licenses Needed:

No special licenses are needed but knowledge of technology and internet marketing is helpful. The most important aspect of an ecommerce business is branding and marketing; so you will need to have strong skills in those areas.

Other Resources:
www.ebay.com
www.amazon.com
www.shopify.com
www.volusion.com

EVENT / WEDDING PLANNER

There are over 2.5 million weddings each year and about $40 billion spent on weddings. If you have experience with planning events or the skills necessary such as organization and creativity then this is a business you can start on the weekends and build.

As a wedding planner you will provide services including:

- Contract management with vendors
- Preview event site to determine needs
- Ceremony and reception program design
- Protocol advice
- Develop timelines, schedules and monitor progress
- Communicate with all participants and service providers to confirm details
- Guest list management and seating chart development
- Wedding rehearsal direction and planning
- Wedding day coordination and management
- Ensure that the events of the wedding and reception run smoothly

A wedding is one of the most important days in a couple's life and with busy schedules between work and other activities more are turning to a professional planner to help their big day. As a professional you must present an image that will make them feel confident that you will be able to create this day for them and ease their preparation burden.

In the beginning you may want to volunteer your services to friends or brides on a budget with their agreement that you can use their wedding to build your portfolio and they will be a reference. When meeting with prospective clients let them know that you will focus on their needs and only book one wedding or event per weekend. Market yourself as someone who provides distinctive weddings or events with style and elegance. Show that you care and will provide outstanding customer service.

Use networking and cross-promotion to find clients; by working with other non-competing wedding professionals you can exchange leads and create joint promotions. These businesses include:

- o   Jewelry stores
- o   Bridal Stores
- o   Florists
- o   Hair stylists / make-up artists
- o   Travel agents
- o   Furniture stores
- o   Real Estate Agents

There aren't any licenses needed however there are certifications and online courses available. And you will need a thorough knowledge of:

- • Event venues and reception sites

Jean Atkins

- Photographers and Videographers
- Flowers / Florists
- Invitations / Stationary
- Music such as DJ's and bands
- Bridal gowns and accessories
- Engagement and wedding rings
- Limousines / Transportation

You will need basic office supplies such as computer, printer and phone; plus you will need a portfolio, business cards and handouts or flyers.

When determining what to charge, there are three ways that planners are paid:

1. Some planners offer "free" service and are paid by vendors with "kickbacks". This occurs when the vendor provides a percentage of the service fee to the planner for bringing them the business. A word of caution: this may inhibit the planner's desire to send you to the best person in the business if the best person in the business is not giving them the highest "kick back".

2. Another form of payment is a percentage fee. Planners using this method generally charge anywhere from 15 - 20% of the total budget for their services. This method is primarily used when a planner is orchestrating an elaborate, large wedding and reception and typically when the event

has a cost of more than $30,000.

3. Other planners offer flat rate fee services. These types of package include a specific amount of hours dedicated to specific activities. Some consider this a better way to go because they feel that the wedding planner will be less inclined to find the most expensive vendors; however a good planner makes it his or her job to keep the bride within her budget. Period. No planner wants to get a reputation of taking a bride outside of her budget on her special day and a good one will work very hard to stay under budget and provide the bride with savings if at all possible without compromising quality and style.

While there are many different methods planners use for fees, you will find that most planners offer packages that include both flat fee and percentage based packages with a variation of services that will suit your bridal needs.

Generally speaking, if you are planning a large wedding with a budget exceeding the national average of $27K you will do better on a percentage fee based package. With flat fee packages there are usually limitations as to how many hours will be dedicated to a wedding with that rate and any hours over that amount are charged at an hourly rate. With percentage based packages there is usually an unlimited number of hours dedicated to this type of wedding and believe me, if it is a large wedding, it will be needed. There are many details to tend to.

Smaller weddings should go with a flat fee

service. There are not as many hours that are needed and a couple could save some do re mi by going this route.

Skills / Licenses Needed:

No special licenses are needed however certifications in the industry will provide legitimacy for your business and confidence with your clients.

Other Resources:

www.bridalassn.com

www.nawp.com (National Association of Wedding Professionals)

www.aacwp.org (American Association of Certified Wedding Planners)

www.acpwc.com (Association of Certified Professional Wedding Consultants)

FITNESS TRAINER OR PERSONAL TRAINER

As a fitness/personal trainer you will assist clients with achieving their health and fitness goals through coaching and training.

Services you can provide are:

- Design fitness programs for you client
- Supervise regular training sessions
- Provide nutrition advice and guidance
- Assist and consult in purchasing fitness equipment

There is a huge market for this service, so many people are struggling to lose weight and willing to pay for assistance. However your target market is those who can afford to pay for this service.

Attract clients by offering in-home services and one-on-one consultations. You can also offer to meet at the client's place of business or at a gym where they have a membership.

In your initial consultation with the client you will want to outline the services you are going to provide and the fees for those services. Have an agreement prepared for them to sign with this and be sure to include a cancellation policy. It is a good idea to collect fees up front, either by the week or month, to ensure your payment but it also helps the client since if it is paid for in advance they are more committed.

Potential clients include:
- Individuals for weight loss
- Businesses to offer as a benefit for employees
- Gyms/Health Clubs
- Retirement communities
- Community Centers

Most importantly, people seeking personal trainers want someone that understands and can sympathize with their plights so you should emphasize your understanding and commitment of each client's needs.

You will want to have some basic and mobile exercise equipment such as floor mats, handheld dumbbells, balance ball, and possibly some yoga equipment. Also if you can provide your clients with supplies such as a food journal will give you and information on nutrition you are providing that extra service.

Skills / Licenses Needed:
Although in general a license is not required to compete in this field you should be certified as a personal trainer; but in certain states licenses or bonds are required.

In addition to being certified it would be beneficial to have knowledge and training in nutrition, plus training in first aid and CPR is an added bonus.

It's also a good idea to be insured to protect you in case of injuries or accidents.

Other Resources:

www.afpafitness.com (American Fitness Professionals & Associates)

www.nfpt.com (National Federation of Personal Trainers)

GENEALOGICAL SERVICES

In this business you will provide a service which researches for ancestry, family history, family tree and storage. Essentially you help clients learn about their ancestors and provide them with an organized breakdown of their family tree.

The information is out there but most people don't have the time or want to take the time to do the research so they are willing to hire someone for this service. If you are good with research and enjoy it then you could make a living at this. First start with your own family, learn how to find the information and go back creating your own family tree to see if this is something you are good at and will enjoy.

Your target market is varied, from individuals to family groups and this can be marketed for family reunions, a gift for family members, a wedding gift; and it makes a great gift for a friend or family member about to give birth.

Skills / Licenses Needed:

There are no licenses or a specific education required; however there are professional genealogists and to compete you may want to pursue educational preparation via institutes and conferences.

Additional tips:

- Determine if you want to price by the hour or a flat fee; when you contract your services with a client get a 50% deposit up front then the balance upon completion.

- Always provide a list of all resources in your report; even if the research turns up no information on the ancestors because anyone who may read the report will know what records had been reviewed so those records would not need to be reviewed again.

- Research on the internet but also use personal contacts in the family or with original records about the client's ancestors.

Equipment and supplied needed include a Soundex system, ancestry maps, genealogy dictionary and of course a computer with internet. Plus other standard office equipment and software to prepare the reports and documents.

Other Resources:
www.bcgcertification.org (Board for Certification of Genealogists)
www.archives.gov/research/genealogy/start-research (National Archives)
www.doi.gov/tribes/research.cfm (US Department of Interior / Genealogical Research)
www.apgen.org (Association of Professional Genealogists)

GIFT BASKET SERVICE

This is a business you can start locally, creating then delivering custom gift baskets. You can create custom gift baskets with items such as flower pots, jams, wines, candies, gourmet foods, fine soaps, cosmetics, jewelry or any specific items the client wants.

Gift baskets are in high demand for birthdays, weddings, anniversaries, graduations, baby showers plus other holidays to target including Valentine's Day, Mother's Day, Father' Day, Easter and Christmas.

Other target markets include corporate offices and businesses; other great contacts are wedding/event planners, florists and real estate agents.

Because there is a great deal of competition in this industry it is a good idea to focus on your local market and promoting your business as one that specializes in unique and distinctive baskets customized to the occasion and to the recipient. This way you can position yourself as a premium gift basket company with superior products and service.

Insider Tips:
- Avoid buying too many supplies or inventory up front; since many of your gift baskets will be custom and specific requests you don't want to spend on building a large inventory. Instead find

suppliers that you can use who will fill your orders quickly.

- Have a plan to meet additional demands during busy times such as holidays.

- Increase profits by offering add-on products that you can up sell to your clients such as personalized gift items, balloons or specialized gift cards.

To promote your business a good, professional website is necessary; as a premium supplier you need to have a premium website showing the amazing gift baskets you can put together. You will also want to network and build strong relationships with local businesses and organizations. Consider offering a gift basket as a prize or door prize for conferences, charity events and large parties to gain recognition and publicity. Other methods for promotion are sending brochures or flyers to local businesses, churches, hospitals, event planners and large organizations. Most cities have various arts and crafts festivals where you can purchase a booth to showcase and sell your baskets. You can also look at participating at flea markets but be careful not to lose your status as an upscale gift provider; but you could offer some discount versions of your gift baskets.

Skills / Licenses Needed:

There are no special licenses needed for making gift baskets; however, you may need an occupational license and in some areas you may be required to obtain a health permit if you are handling and selling food items.

Basic office equipment such as computer, internet, printer and phone are needed plus business cards and flyers/brochures. A good work area with ample space for storage and preparing your gift baskets is beneficial.

For supplies look at Gift Basket Supplies (www.giftbasketsupplies.com) and Wholesale Gift Basket Suppliers (www.giftbasketsuppliers.com).

Other Recourses:
www.GiftBasketBusinessWorld.com
www.giftbasketsupplymarketplace.com

HANDYMAN SERVICE

This is a business growing in rapid demand as more working people need help around the house. Services a handyman provides include:

- Painting cabinets

- Simple plumbing issues such as installing new faucets

- Hanging difficult objects such as large paintings, shelves, etc.

- Assembling items such as furniture

- Moving furniture or heavy objects

- Hanging light fixtures

A handyman can perform hundreds of tasks around the house that elderly or handicapped people need help with also busy executives or people who do not have skills or strength to handle these tasks.

The work is usually done for home owner and also renters but may also include commercial accounts. The most lucrative accounts are with rental agencies, landlords and real estate companies/agents. You will want to convince your prospective clients that you will offer them extraordinary service, convenience and savings. Always be professional, be on time, let the client know that no job is too big or too small and do what it takes to make the client happy.

Promote your business by networking and always ask for referrals. Advertise in local community newspapers and magnetic signs on your vehicle are inexpensive. When you are on a job look around for other jobs needed and offer a special deal to the client to add that on.

Rates you can charge depend on where you live but generally a handyman charges around $25 an hour and up to $50. Check the prices of handyman services in your area.

Skills / Licenses Needed:

For the most part no special license is needed; however, if you do certain kinds of repairs such as electrical or plumbing, some areas may have licensing requirements. And of course you will need to have skills in areas such as carpentry, plumbing, electrical, drywall, masonry, painting and other tasks.

You will need to have basic tools such as hammers, screwdrivers, wrenches, socket sets, drill with concrete and wood drill bits, pliers, wire cutters, tape measure and a tool kit. Additionally it is good to have a ladder, paint supplies and a reliable truck for transporting.

Other Resources:
www.HandymanAssociation.org
www.Handymanaa.org

HOUSE PAINTING

If you have the skill for painting then launching a business providing interior and exterior painting of houses and businesses may be for you.

There is a growing need for house painters as with the other businesses mentioned due to the increase in busy lives and careers. More homeowners and even renters are making improvements to their homes with painting. Also potential clients include commercial businesses plus apartment and property management companies.

Commercial clients have an advantage over private individual homes because if they like your work then it could lead to more business. The constant flow of tenants moving in and out creates consistent work for painting and improvements. However with commercial clients typically you will charge less but receive more jobs; whereas with private individuals you can charge more.

You will want to promote yourself as being skilled in painting, reliable and affordable to compete. In the beginning you can rent additional equipment as needed for each job and be sure to accurately estimate what will be needed for each job. Also have a portfolio of "before and after" photos of jobs you have completed.

Having a truck or van will be beneficial; and other equipment you will need to accrue is:
- Ladders
- Brushes

- Drop cloths
- Painters tape
- Pressure sprayers
- Stir compressors
- Electrical paint rollers

The paint and primer for each job will be purchased per job; you will want to get a deposit up front which will cover the costs.

As your business and reputation grow you can expand and hire painters so there is great potential to make a good income.

Skills / Licenses Needed:

You will want to obtain a professional license to launch your business; you can get this from your state's department of business and regulation (or your specific state equivalent) and is found under the contracting and/or construction area. Once you pass the examination, the state will require you to purchase liability insurance to ensure that both you and your clients are covered in the event of an accident. In many states it is illegal to operate a contracting business of any kind (which painting is) without a state-sanctioned license.

Gaining house painting experience and knowledge is the first step in becoming a licensed paint contractor. There is no substitute for the knowledge acquired through experience. Working under an experience house painter is a great way to sharpen your skills. Pay attention to the business aspects of the job as well.

You will also want to check into the workers compensation requirements in case you are injured on the job; you can do this at www.workerscompensation.com.

Other Resources:
https://www.pdca.org (Painting and Decorating Contractors of America)
http://www.iupat.org (International Union of Painters and Allied Trades)
http://www.thepaintstore.com
http://www.ppgpro.com/painting-supplies-equipment

LAWN CARE / LANDSCAPING

The demand for lawn care and landscaping can be seasonal or in high demand year around depending on where you are located. But even in states where it is more seasonal there are still jobs to keep you busy; and consider all the business parks, apartment complexes, shopping malls and hospitals that need service in addition to homes. Whether it's mowing, trimming, planting, seeding, or during winter add clearing snow and ice...there is always work to be done.

It is easier to break into the residential market than it is the commercial especially starting out when you equipment and capital is limited. So your prime target starting out will typically be residential homes in middle or upper-class neighborhoods.

Focus your promotional material on offering a new client discount and that you provide reliable and quality service. Target homes with large yards which mean bigger jobs with less loading and unloading and less travel time. Advertising can be fairly simple and inexpensive; prepare professional looking flyers or door hangers and leave at the homes in your target neighborhoods. Advertise inexpensively in your community shoppers' guide newspaper, which also helps you target the local area. To gain clients, initially you can offer special pricing or a free additional service, like a coupon for one free snow removal job during the winter months.

Along with your lawn care skills, focus on delivering strong customer service. Providing friendly, courteous service will help you build your business through word-of-mouth referrals. People can be very particular about lawn appearance, so be prepared to go the extra mile to ensure customer satisfaction. When you meet with prospective clients to provide an estimate always present yourself in a professional manner.

You will need a truck and/or trailer to transport the equipment; and the equipment needed include:

- Lawn mower

- Blower and brooms

- Rakes

- Trimmers

- Plenty of water and sunscreen

Consider renting some of the larger equipment as your business grows. Check the cost and availability of local rentals. When buying, look for equipment with good warranties that is easy to service and repair.

Skills / Licenses Needed:

Some states require a contractor's license for landscape contractors and some states require insurance; check with your local government agency. And since this a business where accidents can happen it is a good idea to have insurance and workers compensation.

You will also want to look into regular collision, liability, and damage insurance on vehicles. Get liability insurance to cover damages that may occur during your gardening services.

Other Resources:
http://www.lawnserviceforum.com
https://www.landcarenetwork.org/index.cfm

MOBILE AUTO DETAIL

A mobile detail business will service customers who wish to have their cars washed and detailed at their home or work. The business will provide basic car wash services and more expensive waxing and detailing service.

The average car costs more than $20,000.00 so people are take pride in their car and will spend the necessary time and money to care for it.

Your selling point will be that you provide a mobile service which offers convenience, great service and quality work. Some of the services you will provide are:

- Odor and water removal

- Interior vacuum and cleaning

- Leather cleaning and conditioning

- Pet hair removal

- Exterior wash

Target areas such as shopping centers or malls offering to detail their cars while shopping. Also target office complexes offering to detail vehicles for clients while they are at work. Anywhere that someone may be for a extended length of time is potential target; including movie theaters, you can offer to detail their vehicles while they watch a movie. Work out a promotion with local sports teams to offer mini-details during games.

Skills / Licenses Needed:
No special licenses needed other than local requirements to run a business.
Supplies and equipment needed include:

- Buckets

- Sponges and buffing pads

- Wax

- Sprayers/Pressure foam kit

- Vacuum/blower

Other Resources:
www.autogeek.net
www.carwash.com

MOBILE NOTARY

A mobile notary provides legal, professional and quality Notary Public services to individuals and/or companies by taking your services to your clients.

One example of the kind of work you might do is to be the notary-signing agent who receives loan document papers via mail carrier. You would then meet with the client(s) to go over the loan documents and point the borrower to the signature lines then notarize the documents requiring notarization. Other potential clients include mortgage companies and real estate agents who often have documents that need to be notarized.

Any individual can be a potential client; you can advertise in community papers and online in classified sections, pass out flyers and post them on community boards. You can also look into contracting your services to a large notary firm with a large client base.

In addition to regular notary public services you should promote that you do remote document signing/loan closings, fingerprinting services and many other services that people need notaries for.

There is a large need for notarizations, loan signings and fingerprinting at time and places other than during normal business hours and at normal locations (banks, legal and real estate offices) because many people can't travel to the specific offices during working hours or due to other scheduling conflicts. So you can fill this need with your mobile notary service.

A great target is online lending companies who need local mobile notaries. And if you work for a company get a copy of their contract or information about how they pay notaries and make sure you review it thoroughly before signing up with the company. Many notaries have signed up with companies just so they can start earning money then find out they do not get paid because they didn't comply with the terms of the company contract.

You will need general office supplies such as computer, printer, a cell phone and transportation for your mobile notary business.

Types of documents that need notarizations include:

- Depositions

- Acknowledgments

- Inventory of safe-deposit boxes

- Marriage licenses

- Oaths and affirmations

- Vehicle titles

- Mortgage documents

- Loan documents

Skills / Licenses Needed:

Each state varies but generally notaries must complete a course which teaches the basics of what the law requires you to do. For example in California, every notary public applicant must complete a six-hour approved course of study prior to being appointed as a notary public. But some states only require that you complete an application and provide a bond to become a notary public.

Many states notaries are required to obtain a bond; the bond protects your customers against financial loss caused by your mistakes. Bond requirements vary from state to state.

And Errors and Omissions (E&O) insurance which protects you if a claim is made against you is a good idea. The bond protects the public but the E&O insurance protects you.

Other Resources:
www.nationalnotary.org

PET SITTING / DOG WALKER

The growth of pet-owning homes in the United States has grown tremendously and continues to grow; so does the need for pet sitters and dog walkers. Today's pet owners consider their furry children part of the family and are willing to pay for quality service to help care for them.

Caring pet owners hire pet sitters to care for the family pets because of the extra security and extra attention pets receive with professional in-home pet care. Many pet owners love the fact that by using a professional pet sitter their pet and their home is well taken care of.

In addition to making pet-care visits, pet sitters provide other benefits including picking up mail and newspapers, watering plants and creating crime deterrence due to making the home appear inhabited. These will be features you will want to promote as part of your service.

Pet sitting often requires one to three visits a day to a client's home depending on their requirements; these visits include feeding the pet(s), play time and/or walking, administer medication if needed and handle the household duties. Typically these visits are about 30 minutes each. Another service is overnight visits for an additional fee.

To be successful in this business you must have a love and understanding of pets; having good knowledge about dogs and cats is a plus and will help set you apart from the competition. Another service to provide is a daily journal on your visits for the clients so they know what was going on with their pet while they were away and gives them that added feeling of security. A daily text or email letting them know their pet is safe and secure. Maybe even take a photo of their pet while they are away in a happy situation as a special gift.

This is a business where the schedule is somewhat flexible which could allow you to start it on a part-time basis and build to full-time; as long as your schedule allows you to make the visits when needed.

Your prime market to target are single pet owners who need help, pet owners in apartments or condos who need help due to their work schedule, and pet owners who travel.

Keep your service area to a specific area and not too far, you want to be able to visit several clients in one day without a lot of travel time and expense.

You will need to have a service agreement which describes the services you are providing, the fees and the dates for service; include the names of the pet or pets. Also in each agreement provide space for the client to fill in their contact information, a local emergency contact, their vet or animal clinic and space for any special instructions. These items you will keep on file for repeat customers so they will not need to complete an agreement for every service. It is usually a good idea to collect the fee up front noting in the agreement that if the dates or additional services change then additional fees may be required. And it is also a good idea in the original agreement to state that if you incur any costs such as additional food or vet services then the client is responsible for reimbursing you.

As for supplies and equipment needed a cell phone is a necessity plus business cards and flyers to advertise your business. The investment needed to start this business is minimal. However it will take some time to build up a client base so income in the beginning will also be minimal.

Check pet sitters and pet boarding in your area to find out their prices and services.

Other pet services you can offer include grooming and pet waste cleanup (pooper scooper). Also you can offer a pet taxi service for transporting pets to and from vet visits and grooming appointments.

Skills / Licenses Needed:

A license is not required however it is important to be bonded and insured since you will be providing a service in the client's home plus this provides them with peace of mind allowing you in their home. Also if you are going to be transporting a pet in your vehicle it is a good idea to add commercial auto insurance to alleviate any risk.

Other Resources:

www.petsit.com (Pet Sitters International (PSI))

www.petsitters.org (National Association of Professional Pet Sitters)

PERSONAL ASSISTANT/ERRAND SERVICE (also called a PERSONAL CONCIERGE)

So many people today are just too busy to handle all the chores and details of everyday life especially those that are successful with busy careers. More and more executives and those with financial success are looking for personal assistance however most do not need a full-time assistant so this is where your service becomes needed.

There are many different services you can provide including:

- Shopping

- Running errands

- Pet care

- Paying bills

- Making travel arrangements

- Much more

Your target market is busy professionals who need assistance handling personal errands. Also potential clients are those that are mobility challenged such as handicapped or elderly. Obviously the corporate or wealthy clients will be able to pay higher fees but each client has advantages in terms of profitability for your business.

Although senior citizens and the disabled may not pay as high a fee they are likely to be a continuous source of business and provide referrals.

Knowing that you have two very different types of potential customers it's important that you position your business accordingly. Your selling proposition will vary tremendously depending upon which customers you are targeting.

For targeting your upscale customers you need to customize your marketing and services towards this clientele; you will need to set yourself apart and be able to provide quick service and flexibility. Also you will want to create an image of exclusivity.

For the senior and disabled market you will need to be more cost sensitive and offer reasonable prices. But you can more specific and precise with scheduling such as you will handle the grocery shopping every Tuesday morning. Market your services at senior housing and community services; there are more upscale senior communities which are prime markets.

You will need to have great organizational skills, enjoy shopping and running errands and an understanding of personalities and having patience is beneficial. For your more refined clients having knowledge of the finer things and services is needed.

One benefit of starting this business is it takes very little capital up front; there are not many supplies or equipment needed. You will need a reliable vehicle, a cell phone, business cards and brochures, basic office supplies and a good camera on your phone will be useful if you need to send your client a photo before pur-chase. Also a website is important as your profes-sional clients will expect you to have one.

Skills / Licenses Needed:
There are no specific licenses needed for this service; you will need a driver's license for running errands. Also if you plan on offering ser-vices in clients' homes then getting a bond will provide more confidence for the client.

Other Resources:
http://www.ipsainc.com (Personal Shop-pers Association)

http://www.ncakey.org (National Conci-erge Association)

Check competitor websites under Personal Shoppers / Personal Errand Service / Personal Concierge

PHOTOGRAPHY

The field of photography is wide and competitive. There are a wide variety of players out there, from the part-timers freelancing for the local weekly paper to a few superstars who can command fees of $10,000 per day.

As a home-based photographer, you can work on a broad range of subject area, from wedding photography business, fashion, portraits, underwater, product photography and others. You can be a freelance photojournalist or a publication photographer.

While there are various types of photographic activity, professional photography can be broadly divided into two categories: assignment photography and stock photography.

Assignment photography is any photography commissioned by a client. It covers advertising of products, portraits, weddings, school functions and other images shot on assignment. Most photographers spend their entire career shooting on assignments, as it provides lower financial risk for the photographer. You know that you will get paid, either before the event or after the contract has been satisfactorily completed.

On the other hand, stock photography is photography shot on speculation, in advance of being sold. In going after a "perfect air balloon" shot, photographers may take several dozens, if not hundreds of shots, of air balloons that could be made available at a fair price for generic uses.

These "surplus photos" can then be used in a multitude of ways, in newspaper articles, brochures, calendars, web sites, and many more. Instead of commissioning a photographer, many commercial and educational establishments simply buy stock photographs at a lower-cost.

Your first step, therefore, is to determine whether you will specialize or diversify. I started my first business in photography by first learning the business by getting a job with a school photography company. It didn't pay much but I learned about taking photos, setting up equipment, taking the orders and collecting payments; it was a great learning experience so that I could branch out on my own.

You can find potential clients or jobs by marketing to preschools to do their class photos; or to sports leagues to do their team photos. I knew someone who worked the golf courses and got jobs taking photos of company golf tournements or organized golf events. She would take the photos of each foursome on the first hole then when done she would get the photos processed and framed then hand them out as they were finishing. For these type of jobs you want to collect the money up front.

Then there is portrait photography; since you will probably be working out of your home and not have a studion you can still do portraits on location. Such as in the client's home or a park or at their business for corporate head shots. And there is pet photography which is easiest done at the client's home where the pet is probably most comfortable.

And of course there is wedding photography; I got started by covering the weddings for some family members at no charge as a wedding gift but it also allowed me to build up a portfolio. But with weddings you have to be on top of everything because there is no do-overs, you can't ask the couple to kiss again when they are pronounced husband and wife so you have be skilled and ready to catch all those major moments.

But photography can be a very rewarding business, build your skill and it can be very profitable also.

Skills / Licenses Needed:

First you will need equipment; the equipment you will need depends on your budget, space availability and kind of shoots that you do. List all photographic equipment that you will need for at least a year: cameras, lenses, tripods, filters, electronic flash units, studio lights and stands, seamless paper and other backgrounds, and others. Don't be extravagant, buying expensive but rarely used equipment. Purchase high quality core equipment and sufficient back-up to complete any job. Consider rental sources, particularly for one-time use equipment.

If you want to boost your skills there are online classes such as the New York Institute of Photograpy or many local classes taught at community centers or colleges. Then just work on honing your skill.

Check out the competition by going online and viewing their websites, services offered and pricing. And find a lab you can work with if you will be creating prints; they will need to be quality prints.

Other Resources:
www.ppa.com (Professional Photographers of America)
http://photographyassociation.com/
www.wppionline.com (Wedding & Portrait Photography Association – WPPI)
http://aionline.edu/Photography (Art Institute online classes)

POOL SERVICE

The pool care business has a higher demand in certain states such as California, Nevada, Arizona and Florida and can stay busy all year round. But there are homes with pools in all states plus community pools, apartments, small hotels/inns and also indoor pools that will need to service all year long.

For pool care service, you will usually provide service once or twice a week (sometimes more with commercial accounts) and clean the pool plus check the chemicals and treat if needed. The cleaning and chemical service is easy to learn; if you need training you can offer to service a friend or family member's pool at no charge until you have enough experience.

This is a business you can start on your own then as you add more accounts hire employees to help service the pools so that you can focus on building the business even more.

Your target market are residential clients with pools; in some states it will more affluent homes with pools where as in the states mentioned above the majority of houses have pools. These types of accounts are easier to get so focus on the residential clients first then as you build experience and a reputation you can start focusing on the more lucrative commercial accounts.

You can increase profits by selling your clients additional service items such as floating chlorine dispensers. Another way to increase profits is if you can provide repairs on the equipment plus provide equipment upgrades and renovations.

Maintaining the proper chemical balance in the pool is very important and requires skill and knowledge. The test kits for evaluating the chemical levels in pools are simple, but you'll need to learn how to read the test kit and determine what quantity of which chemicals are required. The failure to keep the chemicals in a pool properly balanced over a long period can result in expensive damage to the pool's surface, so it's important to make sure you know how to keep the chemical balance correct.

You will need the basic pool cleaning equipment including a brush, broom, hose, bucket, a skimmer net, a tile brush and jugs for the chemicals (the same jugs are used over and over by refilling at a chemical supply house after they have been emptied treating pools).

A car can be used but a pick-up truck is helpful to have for transporting your tools from house to house; another option is to acquire a small trailer.

Basic office supplies are needed and you will need to have a billing system in place to bill your clients monthly.

Skills / Licenses Needed:

Licensing requirements vary from state to state. In some states, a contractor's license may be required. But for most states the pool cleaning portion of the business does not require any special license. In some states you may need an occupational license; but only if you have a commercial space.

There are many pool service businesses that work out of their house so you should check with local authorities to make sure you comply with all regional legal requirements.

Other Resources:

http://www.ipssa.com (Independent Pool and Spa Service Association)

http://www.apsp.org (Association of Pool and Spa Professionals)

www.poolandspanews.com

PORTABLE PHOTO BOOTH RENTAL

This is a new feature in high demand for weddings, birthdays, business gatherings and other events. There is an initial investment to purchase the portable photo booth then the cost of operating this business is low. There are vendors who sell the portable photo booth as a turnkey business.

This is a business that requires weekend work since most events are on the weekend. The rest of your time will be spent on marketing and networking.

Your target market is primarily middle-income or up who will spend the money on their parties or events; but you can also offer specials during slow times that make it more affordable for anyone who wants to add this fun experience to their party.

To market your service you can network with event and wedding planners, florists, and bakeries; also market yourself at wedding expos.

This is a business you can start with one photo booth then as you grow you can purchase additional booths and hire help.

Skills / Licenses Needed:

There are no special licenses needed for this business; and no photography skills requires. You will need to have the ability to set the booth up and a basic understanding of the photo technology which most vendors you purchase the booth from will assist with.

Other Resources:

www.freedomphotobooth.com (Freedom Photo Booth sales)

www.mojophotobooth.com (Mojo Photo Booth sales)

*research other vendors

RESUME WRITING

If you have a skill for writing then you could provide a service of preparing professional resumes. Surveys show that most job seekers struggle with preparing a resume. This creates a large market who will pay to have their resume prepared for them.

Your target market is wide and varies; anyone who is seeking employment is a potential client. However it will be those looking for management, corporate or professional type positions that will use your service.

In order to secure the business of the job seeker, you will need to make the job hunters believe that they need a resume service. Let them know that a professional resume will maximize their chances of securing the best job opportunity; that they shouldn't take the chance of using a resume that could sabotage their chances.

Obtaining a job is a very personal and important matter for most people, so you will want to position yourself as a dedicated and caring professional that will provide a service for a reasonable price. Let potential clients know the fee paid to you is very reasonable to increase their value to potential employers.

Ask your clients to keep you informed when they land a job then ask for a testimonial.

You will need a computer, software that will allow you to create resumes, a printer and basic office supplies. A website to show you are a professional will be helpful and once you have testimonials you will want to show them on your website.

Skills / Licenses Needed:

No special licenses are needed for this business or service. As mentioned earlier, you will need to possess a skill in writing and being creative about portraying your clients in the most favorable light to employers.

Other Resources:

http://www.thenrwa.com (The National Resume Writers Association)

http://www.rwdigest.com (Resume Writers Digest newsletter)

TUTORING

The tutoring business is an excellent opportunity for teachers, educators, college students or retirees to instruct students privately in various subjects according to your expertise.

Some of the subjects that are common for tutoring are:

- Foreign languages

- Computers

- Music

- Mathematics

- English

There are many advantages to operating a private tutoring business such as being able to work from home and set your own schedule.

Generally you will help student's complete homework, aid in organizational skills, and provide practice and learning in areas they are weak. The common length of time for a tutoring session is one hour.

During the school year, typical hours for homework assistance tutoring are Monday through Thursdays and from 2:30pm through 8pm although you will find that some families prefer weekends.   There is also tutoring opportunities for students during the summer months for remedial or enrichment tutoring. Plus there is tutoring work for adults who have returned to school available year round.

Your prime target market will be parents of students who are having trouble in school and adults who need or want tutoring in areas such as foreign languages. While the students of families in all socio-economic levels may need or desire tutoring, your client base will be middle to upper class families who will have enough discretionary income to afford your services.

Most tutors have a niche or area of expertise; for example a tutor may do strictly elementary school level reading/writing while another may handle only high school level. Or you may have specific areas of math such as algebra depending on your expertise.

To sell yourself as a tutor you need to position yourself as a tutor and expert in your field; to start out you may need to tutor a couple of students free of charge then you can use them as testimonials to obtain paying clients.

Other ways to show experience are:

- A list of your one-on-one, small group or other teaching experience

- Volunteer teaching you did at your child's school or in a local GED or ESL program

- Any tutoring you did during high school or college such as peer-tutor programs

- On-the-job training seminars you presented or other work related instruction

Some additional tips include:

- Always charge in advance

- Require advance notice for cancellations

- Some tutors use a punch card system, where a parent pays for a certain number of half hour tutoring sessions and can then schedule them later

- Take your resume to each of the local schools from where you want to attract clientele

- Other places to post a flyer or advertise include: dance, martial arts or gymnastics schools; recreation offices for local parks; libraries and book stores

- Basic office supplies are needed and if you will be tutoring in your home then you will want to have a specific area designated for tutoring. Even if it's the dining table you will want to make sure it looks professional. Otherwise if you are tutoring in the client's home then you will need to have dependable transportation and any material needed for the subject you are tutoring.

Skills / Licenses Needed:

There are no state requirements or licensing although most parents won't pay much for a tutor who has less than a four-year degree. Realistically, to be a tutor you should have a degree in the areas you choose to tutor or a great deal of experience.

Other Resources:
http://www.ntatutor.com (National Tutoring Association)
http://www.americantutoringassociation.org (American Tutoring Association)

VENDING MACHINE BUSINESS

In today's busy society, vending machines have found a foothold. They've also evolved. Nowadays, you can get an entire meal out of a vending machine. From department store break rooms to grocery stores to colleges, vending machines are everywhere. However, with new businesses popping up every day, there is plenty of room for a savvy entrepreneur. This business allows you the freedom to start small with money you already have. Avoid taking out needless loans and finance this side job with your current one. Select viable locations for your machines or nab an established route.

Items you will need
- Location

- Presentation

- Contract

- Permit

- Machines

- Bulk food, beverages or toys

- Cooler

Make a list of potential locations and vending options in your area. The possibilities for your vending business are immense. Provide healthier vending food options for local schools. Establish snack and food vending machines in break rooms for an office. Energy drinks are another popular option. Although they wouldn't do well in a high school, they might do well at a local community college or fitness center. Other potential outlets include malls, restaurants, pizza and ice cream parlors, fitness clubs salons, department stores, buffets, hotels, dry cleaners, laundries, bars, flea markets, thrift stores and movie theaters.

Tour potential locations to determine if the business uses a current vending service, the demographic of the clientele and customer traffic. Take the time to observe customer traffic. Higher traffic equates to greater sales. Detail your observations on paper to use in your pitch to the establishment owner.

Develop a personalized presentation to pitch to each owner. Include any specific details about each particular business to further highlight the fact that you have done your research and are serious about your endeavor. Include details about the type of vending machines you believe will do well. Include pictures of the machines, if possible. Don't offer a commission if you don't have to. Leave your brochure or business card. Upon callback, present them with a business contract.

Additional tips:
- Track your expenses to ensure that your business is profitable. Figure in the cost of gas, car maintenance, permits and business insurance.

- Every business should have business insurance. You won't need much. Your current insurance provider may be able to connect you with someone.

- Check your machines regularly. An empty machine won't do you any good. Don't count on the owners to inform that you have your machines are running low.

- In the vending industry, every penny counts. You have to put things in perspective. Your machines may only nab $50 in profit each month. While the vending business can be a lucrative one, each machine can only offer so much in profits. The more machines you have, the greater your income.

- Craiglist.org and Vendingconnection.com are great resources for finding established routes for sale. Thoroughly research the seller and go out on the route with him at least once.

- Find reputable vending machines suppliers. If buying used, ensure that you have someone on hand who can fix the machines. Every day that your machine is out of commission, you are losing money.

- Purchase wholesale food, snacks, beverages or toys for your vending machines. Compare

wholesale prices for online distributors and local wholesale companies. Purchase supplies
and equipment, such as a cooler, a change
counter, a basic tool kit, glass cleaner, towels
and a notepad for documenting how much
candy was sold.

Skills / Licenses Needed:
Contact your county clerk to obtain a sales
tax permit. Vending machine owners are required
to pay tax on sales. And confirm if there are other
licenses needed.

Other Resources:
http://www.vendingconnection.com
(Vending Business Resource Directory)

SUMMARY

With enough ambition we can achieve just about anything. You have several ideas here to choose from now the rest is up to you.

Its important to remember that failure is a part of success; learn from the failures and adjust then move forward. Every successful entrepreneur has experienced failures and setbacks but were not defeated by them.

Learn from your experiences, both positive and negative, and use them to build and grow. There is no reward without some risk, so take this chance and if it doesn't work right away don't give up...push forward and success will come.

You must have confidence in yourself and your business, you must believe in it or it won't work. And you must be willing to work for it, success requires dedication so you will need to find that balance between work and home life.

And as you grow build a reliable network around you, surround yourself with like-minded people who believe in you and what you are trying to accomplish.

Are you feeling motivated and inspired? You have the freedom to choose the kind of business you want, and how far you want to take it. And all that is left is for you to get out there and make your dreams come true.

BUSINESSES YOU CAN START NOW

By Jean Atkins

About the Author

Jean Atkins started her own photography business and grew it into a successful business for many years. After making a hobby out of buying and selling items on eBay she began her own eCommerce store selling photography supplies and building it into an art supply eStore.

To write this book she consulted with many friends and collegues who have their own business for their valuable tips and insights to add to hers.

THANK YOU!

AND GOOD LUCK!!

www.ingramcontent.com/pod-product-compliance
Lightning Source LLC
Chambersburg PA
CBHW051715170526
45167CB00002B/673